More Dancing Shapes: Ballet and Body Awareness for Young Dancers

by *Once Upon a Dance*

© 2020 *Once Upon a Dance*

All book profits will be donated to ballet companies struggling under COVID-19.

All rights reserved. No part of this publication may be reproduced, distributed, or transmitted in any form or by any means, including photocopying, without the prior written permission of the publisher, except in the case of brief quotations embodied in critical reviews and other noncommercial uses permitted by copyright law. Dance teachers are welcome to use images for class instruction; please give *Dancing Shapes* credit. For permission requests, contact *Once Upon a Dance* via www.OnceUponADance.com.

Summary: Aspiring young dancers learn about Konora's ballet journey and explore the shapes she creates with her body. With more than fifty poses to contemplate or re-create, readers develop an eye for detail as they practice ballet technique; explore movement concepts; and increase body awareness, spatial perception, and balance. Ballet vocabulary, gratitude, the value of practicing, and review concepts from the first book weave into this second *Dancing Shapes* volume.

ISBN 978-1-7359844-3-8
Main category: Children's Dance
Secondary categories: Ballet Dance; Dancing Reference; Exercise and Fitness for Children; Children's Books on the Body
Discounts may be available for large-quantity purchases. For details, contact *Once Upon a Dance*.

Back cover photos by Oliver Endahl/Ballet Zaida. Non-credited photos by *Once Upon a Dance*.

All readers agree to release and hold harmless *Once Upon a Dance* and all related parties from any claims, causes of action, or liability arising from the contents. Use this book at your own risk.

First Edition

Other *Once Upon a Dance* books: *Dancing Shapes, Nutcracker Dancing Shapes, Konora's Shapes, More Konora's Shapes*

Thank you

Wade Heninger, Oliver Endahl, Megan Farmer, Heidi Leonard (Dancing Shapes), Stacy Ebstyne, Lindsay Thomas, and Angela Sterling

Everyone who helped improve, review, or promote Dancing Shapes

Hello Fellow Dancer,

I'm so happy to have you along on this dancing journey. Since I have so much to tell you, I've squished at least four books into one.

The first section is about me and my dancing history. *(page 6)*

My story leads us right into exploring imagination and storytelling. *(page 13)*

Please remember to warm up your muscles and body. *(page 19)*

We'll talk ballet terms and learn fancy-French directions, *tendus*, *coupés*, and *passés*. *(page 20)*

Next up, we'll think about shape details as we explore many different ways to pose our arms. *(page 24)*

I've made a pile of dancing shapes on the floor for you to think about and hopefully be inspired to re-create sometime. We'll also play a game to spark your creative choreography. *(page 28)*

If you want even more shapes, there are extras on the opposite page and cover. For an extra challenge, figure out which shapes are duplicates from the story's pages and which are new. If you read *Dancing Shapes*, can you identify a pose we repeated?

If you want to learn more about the French ballet terms, there's a section at the end with translations and how I would pronounce the words. I call the ballet words *fancy French*.

So, are you ready to talk dance? Let's go!

Part One
About Me, Konora

Once Upon a Dance coronavirus paused my dancing dreams, but I kept practicing. I'm happy you're interested in dance, and I hope you'll practice with me. Before we start, can I tell you a little about myself?

I grew up dancing at a small studio called Emerald Ballet Academy. When I was 17, I moved to Salt Lake City, Utah, to be a trainee at Ballet West. Managing online high-school classes, dance classes and rehearsals, and living on my own was a big change. I had to cook and clean and take care of myself, but I enjoyed feeling grown-up.

That summer, I attended Summer Course at Pacific Northwest Ballet (PNB) in Seattle, Washington. It was especially nice to be there because it was the fourth time I'd auditioned for PNB's summer program and the first time I'd been accepted! Sometimes trying something again and again (and again and again) pays off.

At the end of the five-week program, I was offered a spot in PNB's Professional Division (PD). It was hard to choose between PNB and staying at Ballet West, but I decided to pack up all my stuff and move to Seattle.

My experience at PNB was like being an almost-ballerina. While PDs are considered students, they often dance alongside professional dancers in performances.

In *Cinderella*, I danced the part of a fairy attendant.

In *Nutcracker*, I was a snowflake and part of the Waltz of the Flowers.

Everyone who came to see the show loved these bright colors. Do I look like a flower?

Left photo: Megan Farmer. Right photo: ©Angela Sterling. Thank you, Pacific Northwest Ballet.

We even had our own Professional Division show. PNB company members I'd admired for years created dance pieces for us to perform. Do you think you would enjoy dancing on this big stage?

Many dancers choose not to perform. Maybe they don't enjoy the pressure of performance, or maybe they want to teach or create dances instead.

Dance   is   for   everybody!

Photo: Lindsay Thomas (Image partially blurred for student privacy). Thank you, Pacific Northwest Ballet.

These pictures are from my first performance. We didn't get to do my last show. That show and most of our job auditions were cancelled because of the coronavirus. In fact, many ballet companies shut down for an entire year.

Left and top photos: Lindsay Thomas.
Thank you, Hayley Majernik and Pacific Northwest Ballet.

I had danced in Ballet Idaho's *Nutcracker*, and they invited me to come back. So after a COVID spring and summer dancing in my parents' garage, I moved again! This time it was to Boise, Idaho.

What a weird time. Because of the coronavirus, we had to wear a mask every day, and could only dance with a small group of people we called our *pod*. Pod is kind of a funny word. It reminds me of dolphins and whales.

Photo: Oliver Endahl/Ballet Zaida

Dolphins and whales make me think of leaping, or *saut de chat*, one of my favorite ballet moves.

Saut de chats are a great example of how some of the hardest ballet moves build from simpler steps. *Saut de chats* (or *grand jetés*) work best if you've practiced *grand battements*, which are harder than *dégagés*. *Dégagés* progress from *tendus*, and we'll work on those in a moment. Even if these fancy French words are new, hopefully you understand how the skills stack up. This picture depicts years of ballet lessons and practice to get stronger, more flexible legs.

Whenever someone in our pod got even a tiny bit sick or knew someone who was sick, we practiced and learned choreography over the computer on Zoom for a few days.

Have you ever learned things from someone far away over the computer?

It's nice to stay home for a day or two, but after a while I'd miss people and dancing in bigger spaces.

I would also miss the sturdy bars from the studio. Holding onto something for balance gives dancers time to improve their shape details.

Photo: Oliver Endahl/Ballet Zaida

Part Two
Imagination and Storytelling

While I was stuck in my bedroom, I thought about how nice it would be to make up my own dancing stories that take place out and about in the wide world. Here are some examples of my dancing daydreams:

What if I could be friends with a magic talking horse getting ready to ride off in search of dragons?

What if I was actually a wish fairy named Wishteria, and I could catch bubbles and turn them into **w i s h e s**?

I thought up those stories for fun, but when dancers learn the steps of a dance, they often create stories for themselves to make their dancing feel more real.

We do this even when a dance doesn't have a story plot.

What do you think is going on in this picture? Can you make up a story to go with it, just to make it more interesting?

What if I dressed myself up with a mermaid tail?

Or put a dragon on top of my feet?

Does that change or influence what you think the story could be about?

Telling stories in our imagination helps us create characters and makes our dancing more meaningful. Sometimes we are told our character and story. In that case, it helps to imagine even greater detail about that character, like what they ate for breakfast, or how they acted with their brothers and sisters.

Dance-creators, called choreographers, also think about costumes and jewelry when they are telling their stories. If they are lucky, they work with a costume designer who helps develop their costume ideas, and a set designer who plans what else goes on stage with the dancers. Those elements make the character clearer for both audience and dancer.

Have you ever worn a costume to help tell a story? Here's me playing dress-up in purple sparkles. In the picture, I'm doing a *passé*, which we'll get to in the next section.

Photo: Wade Heninger/Heninger Fotographik.
Thank you to Emerald Ballet Theatre, Katie, Angela, and Cathy for so many gorgeous costumes.

Of course, before you're ready to put on a fancy costume for a big show, it helps to learn some basics.

I've taken ballet class almost every day for as long as I can remember.

In those classes, we make many of the same ballet shapes and movements over and over. I bet I've practiced my dancing shapes over

5,000 days so far.

Let's get to some ballet basics next.

Warming Up

It's a good idea to warm up your body and muscles before you dance. Here are some ideas:

1) If you know some ballet basics, do *pliés* and *relevés* in *first, second,* and *third positions.* If not, simply bend and straighten your knees ten times.

2) Give all of your parts a gentle jiggle or shake:
- your hands
- your arms
- your feet
- your legs
- your head
- your shoulders
- your back

3) Reach up high, then bend over and try to touch the floor.

4) Draw ten circles in the air using your shoulders as your paintbrushes.

5) Draw circles using each elbow as a paintbrush. Make five little ones and five big ones with each elbow.

6) Draw five little and five gigantic circles with each hand as your paintbrush.

7) Do the same thing with your feet, using your paintbrush toes.

8) Run in place, lifting your knees extra high.

(*We practiced* pliés, relevés, *and the positions in the first* Dancing Shapes *book.*)

Part Three
Ballet Positions

Photo: Stacy Ebstyne Photography

Ballet has many fancy-French words to learn, not only positions and movements, but also related concepts like directions. These French words can be tricky to say and remember, so we'll only learn a few today. The direction our feet move toward could be:
- *devant* (to the front)
- à *la seconde* (to the side)
- *derrière* (to the back)

These pictures are all of *tendus*. In general, *derrière* is the hardest; the secret is to hardly have any weight in the back foot, as if you could lift it up in the air.

Tendus help our feet and ankles get warmed up.

The other ballet terms for today all help us practice balancing on one leg. *Coupé* is low and *passé* moves higher up. We connect the toes of the foot off the floor to the other *standing leg*. With *coupé*, the *working leg*, the leg off the floor, stays near our ankle. With *passé*, the toes (especially the big toe) touch the other knee. With ballet, most of time we're *turned out*, but let's start in *parallel* as it's a little easier.

Coupé in parallel (flexed hands)

Passé in parallel (flexed hands)

For *turned out coupés* and *passés,* the position could be *devant* or *derrière.* Does this pose have a *coupé devant* or *coupé derrière?*

Coupé derrière with standing leg in plié

Coupé devant with standing leg in plié

Sur le cou-de-pied is very similar to *coupé* except the foot wraps around the ankle with the heel in front and the toes in back. Find *sur le cou-de-pied* with a flexed foot, heel in front and wrap your toes around the back of your leg like a snake.

With *passés*, you want your toe to barely touch your leg to make a big triangle while keeping your heel forward and your hips even as they were in *sur le cou-de-pied*.

Sur le cou-de-pied

Passé devant

We'll add *tendus* and *passés* to our next warm-up list. They are a great way to get our muscles ready for harder steps and poses, and you will see both in almost any ballet class.

Part Four

Thinking about Details

With those *tendus* and *passés,* we were pretty focused on our legs. Let's take some time to think about all the small details we can have with our arms, elbows, wrists, hands, thumbs, and fingers.

It's really helpful to make the shapes yourself so you can feel them in your body. Most dancers find it helps us remember if we make movements with our feet or hands while we are learning dance steps.

You could copy these shapes on your knees, standing, or sitting, as we're just thinking about arms for the moment. Watch for curved, bent, or straight arms, and see if you can find any examples of flexed or extended hands.

(We explored curved, bent, straight, flexed, and extended in the first Dancing Shapes *book.)*

• Are my arms and hands exactly the same on each side? If so, we call this symmetrical. If the sides are different, they are asymmetrical. These words can refer to parts or the whole of a shape.

• Are my elbows bent? How much? When it's just a little, we get a curved shape. I can make curves with my wrists as well.

• Where are my palms, the inside of my hands, facing?

• Which way do my fingers point?

• Are my fingers together or separated?

• Do any fingers move in a different direction?

Part Five
Dancing Shapes on the Floor

Photo: Oliver Endahl/Ballet Zaida

Even though I've studied ballet and other dance styles for many years, one thing I wish I'd had more practice with is moving on the floor. When you learn ballet, there aren't that many steps that take you onto the floor. But when choreographers create dance, they often move dancers to the floor because it brings variety. It makes dance more exciting if you have a whole new direction, down and up, to travel.

Practically anything can be a dancing shape, and choreographers often try to create new shapes because they like unique steps and poses, even when they use ballet technique as a starting point.

As you re-create or think about these shapes, think about each component or piece of our bodies, the way we thought about our arms' details. Look for symmetry (symmetrical components or whole shapes).

If you're not sure how to start, maybe begin with the feet or hands. Any task is easier if you break it down into smaller parts.

Now that you've worked so hard copying my shapes, I thought it would be fun to help you create some. Sometimes I play a game where I challenge myself to make shapes with certain body parts connected to the floor. Will you try with me?

Can you create a couple different shapes that have both feet and both hands touching the ground?

Here are a bunch of my ideas. I've left them here in case you want to come back another day and try the shapes I made to get more practice looking at details and replicating dancing shapes.

Ready for more?
- How about a pose with both of your knees and both of your hands touching the ground?
- How about one with your knees and your elbows touching the ground?

I'll put my shapes on the next page, but I want you to try it first.

Great! Next, let's try:
- your bottom and one foot, and then
- your bottom and one hand.

Can you challenge yourself to make different shapes than mine?

Ready for some harder ones? My brain is getting a little tired coming up with all these new ideas. Are you still with me? You can always take a break if you need one.

How about:
- two hands and one foot, and then
- both hands, one knee, and your head?

Again, I'll put my ideas on the next page so you can try it first.

Okay, the next one is difficult to do, but easier to think about. What about balancing on only your bottom?

How could we balance with
no bottom,
no feet,
no hands,
no knees,
no elbows,
and no head ?

Hmm, I suppose my bottom is still touching the floor? Well, sometimes you try something and it doesn't quite work out, and that's okay.

Did you come up with an idea?

Let's finish up with two super-hard-to-do ones. I only made my ideas for these poses for an instant:
- only your heels (the back part of your foot), and then
- only your knees.

Phew! That was a super challenge. I wish I could give you a high-five.
I am totally giving you a high-five in my imagination right now!

I hope you enjoyed making these poses. If you want an extra activity another time, come back and make up stories for some of these crazy poses you or I made up.

Maybe making these shapes was difficult today. Like everything, if you come back another time, it will be easier. Everything gets easier with practice. Most things worth trying are worth practicing. You know what, I still have to practice almost every day. How crazy is that? It's a good thing I love to dance.

I also want to say it's okay if you don't love dance as much as me. I hope someday you find something you love to do as much as I love dance, but you have plenty of time. At your age, it's fantastic to try different things and learn what makes you happy, what makes you jump for joy.

Hey, look, nothing's touching the floor 😏!

Thank you for playing my silly game and for working your body and brain.

Keep learning.

Keep trying.

Keep practicing.

Stay safe.

Until our next adventure,

Love, *Konora*

P.S. What do you think I'm holding? I'd love for you to make up a story about this picture. You could even have your grown-up send it to me at *www.OnceUponADance.com*.

Fancy French*

- saut de chat ['so-deh-SHAW'] jump of the cat
- grand jeté ['grawn zhuh-TAY'] big throw
- grand battement ['grawn baht-MAHn'] big beat (might also hear *grand battement jeté*)
- dégagé ['day-gah-ZHAY'] to disengage   (might also hear *battement dégagé* or *battement jeté*)
- tendu ['tawn-DOO'] stretched (might also hear *battement tendu*)
- devant ['duh-VAHn'] in front
- à la Seconde ['ah-la-say-KON'] to second (movement that goes side)
- derrière ['deh-REE-air'] behind
- coupé ['KOO-pay'] to cut
- sur le cou-de-pied ['sur-leh-koo-deh-pee-AY'] on the neck of the foot
- passé ['pah-SAY'] passed

  passé is the movement, *retiré* is the position, both words are used
- retiré ['reh-tee-RAY'] withdrawn
- plié ['plee-AY'] bend (bent/bending)

Concepts Review
- standing leg and working leg
- curved arms and curved hands
- symmetrical/asymmetrical
- connection to the floor

Coming Up Next
We're working on a couple of books. Grown-ups can subscribe at *www.OnceUponADance.com*. (Watch for subscriber bonus content.)

Not official pronunciations.

Photo: ©Angela Sterling

We'd jump for joy and really appreciate a grown-up's review at Amazon or Goodreads.

We're a mom-daughter pair who were both happily immersed in the ballet world until March 2020. It took a lot of learning and a lot of practice to create *Dancing Shapes* and *More Dancing Shapes*.

It would mean so much to us if you'd let us know you enjoyed them. While we are unable to perform or watch a performance, a positive review is our applause.

Check back for more books from *Once Upon a Dance*.

Once Upon a Dance was created during COVID-19. It started with videos encouraging kids stuck at home to join ballerina Konora for movement and dance for exercise and meditation.

Konora is a trainee at Ballet Idaho.

Konora's mother taught creative movement and ballet for twenty years and was honored to be chosen and recognized by her local City Council for "embodying the spirit of partnership and commitment to children in our community" for her work with young dancers.

Visit www.OnceUponADance.org for free kids' content.

Visit www.OnceUponADance.com to subscribe and for information about *Once Upon a Dance* books:
Dancing Shapes
Konora's Shapes
More Dancing Shapes
More Konora's Shapes
Nutcracker Dancing Shapes

Made in the USA
Monee, IL
13 March 2021